Fish Guts

by Lisa Thompson
illustrated by Steven Hallam

⊆Harcourt Achieve

Rigby • Saxon • Steck-Vaughn

www.HarcourtAchieve.com
1.800.531.5015

Characters

Liam

Kelly

Dad

Contents

Chapter 1

Fish Food

Dad opened the box of fish bait. "Which one of these will the fish want to eat today?"

"What do you think, Liam? Do you want worms, fish guts, or shrimp heads?"

"Fish guts, thanks Dad," I said as I set up my fishing rod. Dad passed me a little box of bait.

6

"Kelly, how about you?" asked Dad.

"I think I'll have worms," said Kelly.

"That leaves me with the shrimp heads," said Dad.

"Phew," Kelly said. "This stuff stinks. I can't believe fish like to eat this stuff!"

She picked up a worm and wrapped it
around her hook. I did the same with
my fish guts.

10

"Hey, Kelly! How good does this look?" I dangled my hook in front of her. It was loaded with fish guts.

"Not as yummy as my juicy worm!" Kelly said, holding up her hook.

"OK, you two," said Dad, "time to cast out."

Chapter 2

Casting Out

We had to try a few times. It was hard to cast our lines out far enough.

"Now all we have to do is wait for the fish to bite!" Kelly said.

"When they smell my fish guts, they'll swim in from everywhere!" I said loudly.

We sat down and waited. We waited and waited.

Dad had a little bite and reeled in his
line. There was no fish on the end of it.

Kelly felt something, but it was just a weed.

I didn't even get a bite.

"It must be the bait that you're using," teased Kelly.

I was just about to pull in my line when
I felt it. There was a tug on my line.
Then I felt another . . . and another.

Suddenly my line went tight. "I've got a bite!" I shouted.

Chapter 3

On the Line

My fishing reel was spinning. The fish was swimming off with the bait.

"Reel it in!" yelled Dad.

I held on tightly to my fishing rod.
I tried to wind in my line. This fish was
strong. I could barely hold on.

I was winding in as fast as I could.
Then I saw the fish. It was the biggest
fish I'd ever hooked.

"Get the net, Kelly," Dad yelled with excitement. "It looks like a big one!"

Suddenly *snap!* My line broke. The fish
was free. My line was empty. My hook
and my fish guts were gone.

"Never mind," said Dad.

"Yeah, plenty more fish in the sea," laughed Kelly.

I wasn't worried. I knew where my fish had gone. He had swum back to tell his friends about the best fish guts he'd ever tasted.

All of them would want some. He would bring the whole school back with him, and I'd be here waiting. Ready with hook, line, and tasty fish guts for them all!

Glossary

bait
food used to catch fish

cast out
throw a line into the water

dangled
hung loosely in the air

fishing rod
a pole used to catch fish

reel
part of a fishing rod
that pulls in the line

school
a group of fish

spinning
turning quickly

wind
twist around
something

Lisa Thompson

Some goldfish love eating boiled lettuce and peas. Yuck! You need to cook the peas until they are soft, and then mash them with your fingers before serving. One pea is usually plenty.

If I were a fish, I would easily be caught hook, line, and sinker with a piece of chocolate. How about you?

Steven Hallam